Hazards of Enlightenment

Dianne Aslett

Hazards of Enlightenment

Published by RedSox Press 2017

www.redsoxpress.co.uk

ISBN 978-0-9935355-3-6

RedSox Press Limited Reg. No. 09863441

Printed by CreateSpace

For My Mother & Father

To all of those who live 'on the edge', and whom, through being endlessly forced to take risks to seek some kind of balance, --and then sometimes falling – often find themselves hanging on by a mere thread. As many such people have discovered, a dire position can – however frighteningly – result in amazing 'finds'. Most shockingly, in one's finding, in that very moment, the 'Pearl of Great Price'.

Dianne Aslett
Spring 2017

Contents

The Egg I live In

The egg I live in
waits in shadow –
how long I've lingered
I can't say –

Its shell is crackable
I feel the sharp stings –
the all-too vivid light.
I hunch up my shoulders –
soothe my soul –

World within worlds
sisters' habits enthral
Holy Grail –
wrap around me,
me, fermenting foetus –

I feel fragile –
glowing under moons –
nourished by darkness.
Beyond the muffled sounds
the clock can't stop.

Where Are You Going?

When they call
you know you must have
an answer, a plan,
a convincing biography,
a name

a point of view
a reason why you came

— and that is all?

Forgetfulness

What to remember?
Essence that dreamt
its way into Incarnancy
— or
the fastest route to Watford...?

Hazards Of Enlightenment

As the Buddhas-in-waiting sit upon the sands
behind the curtains are hidden your hands.

And the clown-on-stilts mimics the trawl
of the ocean's relentless push and pull.

Children's squeals evoke the Holy Ghost
as the glinting kites approach their Host.

The signs glow bright but too loud for most
for the casino's bandits control the coast

and the random dog stoops low to bark,
returns brave waves back to deep and dark.

For the Buddhas-In-Waiting who sit upon sands
behind the curtains, rarely see your hands.

The Icon

Don't touch.

The gold comes off
when you touch.

I wondered why
I was always
getting smacked...

Truth costs
such a lot,
doesn't it?

In other people's houses,
you must
not
notice the dust. (Just
let it settle).
Be Good, Keep Quiet. And,

DON'T TOUCH!

Who do you think you are,
anyway? ----

God?

(Ouch!)

Wisdom

The wise way
is the letting be
of the world in me,
of the witness to wonder
at the thousand things.
To know beyond mirage
to penetrate the façade
to intuit and conduit
Beauty.   Light —

to know
you are nothing.

'Trajectories' for D.W.

If mirrors are all, are all we have
then energies generally play games
and if we interfere to choose the names
of things, still they remain
mirrors of all and only that we have.

If mirrors are all, are all we have
then your betrayal is simply my own,
a self-destructive intent that I have grown
because I choose blame
and punish as if my death I crave.

If mirrors are all, are all we have
then my own gestation was groomed
out of the unborn Divine I sought a room
a mere rearrangement of atoms,
new possibilities to misbehave.

If mirrors are all, are all we have,
something beyond must tweak me
provide the empty sky in which can see
the chaos and the harmony,
gangplanking nonsense, gloriously ecstatic,
even beyond the grave.

Today

Today the psyche affluent
ran less hinderedly
criss-crossing yours,
angles obtuse, scalene,
right-angled, obscene,
an embrace not seen before.

Today I didn't dribble round
you, or palm hard your back,
or trip your leg; wore
my fantastic fantasies
loosely in the breeze
of your open window. Saw

the potency of truth,
instead of circling Indian-style,
your stagecoach, I trotted
firmly to your centre, cool,
and I think we may,
just may
have touched my soul
today.

Unleashed

I am wanting to see the Light
but the darkness
--A black cat
is creeping,
its eyes boring into me
up to the undercarriage
of my chin.

I am wanting to see the Light
but the terror
in my belly
upon awakening
for months now
belies my quest
shiveringly.

I am wanting to see the Light
but the portents
of appeasement
splutter my guts
and the insect drones
already in sight
are stealing our sky.

Hidden Blessings

You stole my mum
and left me glum
and when I didn't know
I couldn't grow ---

And the anguish slept
though I often wept
and as I begged for more
the less I saw ---

And the 'powers that be'
they surrounded me
but made their demands
amidst closet palms ---

Now the game's been rumbled
the artifice crumbled,
I understand the trend
and the route to mend

the orphan's misery

is mankind's history
and the mum I thought
was the prime stalwart
is the shadow and strife
of the main midwife,
not the Source at all
not at all, at all...
but the Crane's blest call....

And I couldn't grow
'cos I didn't know
and they left me glum
when they stole my mum

Oh, so slow to learn
that one must Return
to the sheltering claw
where need's no more...

And to let go, give up
but keep clasping the Cup...

Shaking Hands

Where are your hands?
Naked and nude?
I see Buddha
I want you rude.

Where are your hands?
And the shining flesh?
I see Buddha
I want you fresh.

Where are your hands?
Let your hiding cease,
I see Buddha
I want your peace.

Where are your hands
Your mind would destroy?
I see Buddha
I want your joy.

Where are your hands
Please take off your gloves,
I see Buddha
The Being Who Loves.

Protocol

Something has changed.
The constraints of black,
chain us,
the protocol of charred wood,
of lives profoundly burnt and burning.

Can I catch
the authentic
beyond the deep, dark hush?

The studied, avoidant stares
the evocative thud,
the concise and solid prayers?

What can be said
that rightly honours the Dead?

Beyond the craft,
the magick

of the odd and awkward word,
the silent signal

of something unsayable...?
'She's in a better place', you say.
'She was in so much pain'.

And I'm ashamed to acknowledge the sham
but I nod
and a wan smile
dutifully mirrors your sentiment,
stifling my urge to shatter it---

Since I too yearn for the Empress' arms
and the 'happy ever after'...
But the light and the love and the bliss
I know will not be like this---
for surely the forms will be missing...

And truly
we cannot know.

And maybe,
neither does it matter?

So.
My question remains:

must I cry, also,
in the weird draught

of the raft, — the sudden suck
of bad luck

and this solemn drift?

(Or can I, as with most things,
exempt myself?)

The Kill

I walked leisurely through a field
long leaning blades of green
surrounding;
a shield
unsheared; I plucked
a tiny strand
began to sing
and by the stream
I sucked
and thought: this land,
deprived of man, this thing,
flourished. I caught
a passing glimpse to fold
into You, God, and wished
to be near, forever
but
I wouldn't learn.
Sold
to self
I never
knew

for, I couldn't hold
or fence your wealth
but yearn;

and when you said

'I'm here'

 each
 sense, in turn,

went

 dead.

Waiting

I'm here, behind the veil,
waiting. The Other
hides, I don't know why.
I'd like our finger tips to touch,
to excite, to see the light.
Not by, or through,
but to see You
and to be
You.

Where the veil is split
the time is ever now.

If you get out,
will you show me how?
Will you come back,
down in to the black sky,
and get me?

Winter

Winter holds fast, trees

shocked and comfortless,

the Sisters of Mercy, black statues

bent

in prayer.

Christmas Landing

Here I am
at humanity's head
in surreal 3D
striding down the street

I have eyes
I have feet.

Here I am
with a mind and a will,
I am solid and strong
strangely focused yet wild:

The Incarnate child
set loose on the world.

Christmas Poem
December, 2012

This morning
I am eating god for breakfast.
This morning
I will give god a bath

And the world will
glow
gold
with my aura
burning
the ancient dust.

And the dervish ego
turned out...
out-side-in,
in-side-out

turning
so 'there' becomes 'here'
as he goes

round and round--
throwing off his crust

--tearing off the stale,
biting his tail.

This morning
I am eating god for breakfast.

Jesus

I've thought a lot
about this —
What a clot
I was
to challenge Pilate
with such disdain,
to go to the Garden, alone-
Iscariot's cheeky
opportunism.

I've pondered and I've pondered
as to how I squandered
my Message's Mission,
the cross-hatched frisson

wasted

in Time...

the populace's
turning tide,
their stomach's contempt,

hell-bent
on bread and wine....

I should have
wooed the rich more,
shared Buddha's palace,
ignored the miscreants,

favoured my mum...

taken out Life Insurance,
invested more wisely...

— Been A Tory.

Outcomes to SAQ

To carve a life
in Truth,
I've splattered and I've spluttered
with the worst of them (who shan't be named),
and with the best of them,
who shall be:
Rajneesh, Krishnumurti, Jesus & Mohammed.
I've wondered and I've wondered,
starved and over-filled,
been tortured and been taunted,
excited and exhausted.
Ridden night-mares,
head-less and undaunted,
or the cupped coward in some Masadan cave.
I've been kind; I've been candid; I've been rancid.
I've flown high, and later landed.
And sometimes,
— perhaps 3 times in a lifetime?
I've walked on water.

Deep Down

Deep down the doubt
Continues:

the BBC News
does it
the Christians
do it
the Muslims...

But deep down, the doubt
continues...

Intellectuals everywhere
do it.
The Tories do it.
Labour does it.
The Communists
the Fascists
— They all do it.

But deep down, the doubt
continues...

It isn't News.

There is no 'News'.

In the end
you have to
eat it,
so it
runs through
your body-and-your-blood,
till it hijacks
your bones

and carries you home.

Trapped

That mouth-hole
of death,
once known
never leaves you
alone.

It sucks and smacks
like a lizard's
lunging
tongue
tugs
and clings

relentless and true.
Proferred chase
will someday
bring him back
running rings
round you.

You have to release
and fall, let go

when
he calls
you have to
Enter
backwards.

The Rebels

Give me freedom
says the youth.
Let me out
so I may shout
the Truth.

Give me freedom
says the child.
Abolish schools
and their rules
run wild.

Give me freedom
says the soldier.
Let my bravery
be blood-red
bolder.

Give me freedom
says the pop-song.
Allow me all
so I may call

nothing wrong.

Give me freedom
Says the undergrad.
Little seeing
in his being

'where

   it's

      at.'

Swords

My values are as good as yours –
therefore,
we are equally acceptable,
and neither needs to change.
And I can dance
and you can dance
world-wild and free.
It is the only way
to be happy.
No more judging then,
for,
they who judge,
judgement shall return to them,
piercing your own heart.

My values are as good as yours-
and this is me. ('and me and me')
this is the only way to be.
So Drink This Cup

Wake Up!

Night Out

Thrust forward the dark trust
in the abandonment of incarnation
the self-blinder digs deep,
heaves dirt out into the sky.
— And so sucks the black hole
of forgetting
there is no control —
only Light beckoning
without cause or intent.

Prolonging The Yawn

However fast you run
you never reach.
Hope, the horizon,
ever recedes.

Bored, I am,
with the omnipresent screen.
the shuffle and careen
of the toddler's scam.

The pretence of the creator
the fiendish impersonator
the requirement to fawn.

To justify one's mission:
the continuous production
of apples, GM'd –

So we can guarantee
the cascade
repeated and eternal
upon our heads

providing the need
to bruise
and dramatize
and bleed

before maturity can dawn.

Priest

For B.B.

There is an aching void
I cannot bridge
and the breach
echoes
the universal
horror:
the angst and the absurdity
the iron wall
of necessity
we must all
pass through some time
(It is The Fall).

Yet wrapped in Him
love conquers all
The Final Fling –
The First Man and The Last.

We crucify all reconcilers
like grapes are crushed for wine
and bread

must be broken
to be shared.
Then, and only then
Life rises from the Dead.

(You see, I really cared –
THAT'S why I dared.)

Amen. Amen. Amen.

Getting Earthed

It's only post-ontologically that I hate you; if
Adam'd not sinned, in amniosis still
I'd float with you, glow transparently,
replete with heaven.

It's only post-ontologically that I hate you; from
One: two, three, then earth was filled,
dense energy birthed egos, eternity
kick-started some kind of leaven.

It's only post-ontologically that I hate you; when
earth's hybrid atoms stirred this strange crucible,
so now, Eden echoes as a land of fantasy,
and St. Paul's transport to Star-day-scare Seven:

another tale-trail confabulating skies; then
clues misunderstood, misread
in Bibles, Gitas, Korans, Kabbalahs, —
in all Mysteries, tributaries dance and bleed.

On Life And Death And Suicide

There is already enough war in the room.
Let us burn together; --- I yearn
for us to burn together, and go home.

Even in your pain, I'd like you to know
The Light that you are,
that I am.   And so I touch you
and in the darkness we can feel
All Of It.
And not escape — but be thrillingly real.
Even, and maybe only,
through the brave fires of hell —
The ache to return to what was always beckoning:

ever the vastness of the Ocean, its frightful surge,
mightily eternal, the Matriarch,
cradling the peek-a-boo, chattering wave.

Fire and Water...

Nothing Further To Add

Poem for B.B. with love

Ensconced in rationalism

so secure

an indefinable nag

tugs

towards the

emptiness of his stomach.

We had

so much in common

-the escape from angst-

my deviance

only a question

of mode —

'cept strangely I feel blessed.

And Love – what about 'Love'?

The vision lifts,

uplifts.

planets ahead

they will receive me,

— and so will you.

Loss

The incarnate stript,
each and every bit,
day by day my death
by stealth you seize my breath.

Physique and will and want
and earth and bird, who haunt
dreams that are my script
So relentlessly I'm stript.

A belly sucked arid,
aches like Armageddon.

Even the kiss,
(the utterly kind kiss),
love's dove fledged ---
meets the empty sky.

Limbo

Everything Moves,
but the Glue's
Fast.

Djinn at loose,
skip in and out
my grave.

Alive or Dead?

It's An Open Secret

Transcendental makes my soul soar,
pushes through and beyond, the core
encircled by a quillion separated visions
and dreams.

Transcendental excites my five-foot-seven,
quickens this blood, and every sense that's given
immortal kudos to my mission
on this ordinary earth.

Transcendental floods my mind and heart with joy,
reminds this Child of God that Life's quite serious toy
is built with humorous precision
as crystallised mystery.

Imbalance

A chasm displaced then, now
your boundaries prevent the flow

and I, I do not know, now,
the name you legally acquired
---or the qualities, expired.
I know not now,
how the tricks, the spell
could blind us all
so completely.

The games you played
the love, the trust, seduction,
the deep, dark wood
that led me to believe in good,
now,
I cannot return.
I no longer know.

But only gape before the chasm,
the unholy rape
of tender film that protected me
so loyally till then,
when the boundaries dissolved
at your bidding
----but never mine.

I Came Looking

I came looking for you
between a multitude of wrappings
inside that great womb
where you were protected.

I came to you in search of succour
half-expecting to find you sleeping
as they had said...
but there you were awake,
and waiting for me.

Available and ample.

Burning Bush

You think the Sage is full of love--
everything mellow moods dream of,
defending beauty, joy and peace,
the weak, the good, promoting feasts...

You think the Sage is full of pleasant
likes order, clean and without want,
no nasty horrors can really blast,
your safe and cosy life will last.

You think the Sage will keep the pledge
and never push you o'er the edge,
but listen: the Sage Is more unkind
than any merely human mind.

Listen: Your death will creep and spring,
destroy each common familiar thing,
your body will rot, the earth to clog,
your person less sacred than a stuffed straw dog.

Defiance

The sun I will not give you
because like a leather hide I'm stretched beneath it
the sun I will not give you
until you show me your burning hand.

Then we may dance together
under the moon
skip on the water
as we mirror our shadows.

The sun I will not give you
until you show me your burning hand.

Nothing Sucks

Nothing is happening,
just the split of your projectiles,
and mine.   As we create time,
even resonate
in rhyme —
as if the symbolism of style, individual or replicant
like the ant which guests a while
in its soldier's role,
busy and bothered — carries the heavy world.

And what of desire?

Its earthiness, deep in the earth's guts,
leaping as fire, sticking and licking, its curl
slithers like the serpent circling this banker's bucks.

All is unreal,
whatever you feel, see, hear, smell —
we shriek at the 'Bell'. Yes, it's good ol' Death —
we return to our Source
to the hub and the core — where the apple's no more.

Dust to dust as before, yes,
prior to all crime.

No, Nothing is happening
but the Void, birthing Time —

nothing Sucks.

Eye

Me, Nucleus, sleep, as Galileos'
copious notes scribe journals
in cyber-space; history's famous telescopes
tunnel back the star-years as each hurls
the Romans into theological fury.

Me, Nucleus, sleep, Heisenberg's
theory can't truly measure me,
as the Black Swan wraps its soft-word
-wings around my loaf-soaked anonymity,
electrons orbit, spin-dizzy, blurry.

Me, Nucleus, sleep, as astral travel,
I heal the oak's bark, the willow's leaves,
the kid's kinder helicopter hard to unravel,
clings to the icy branches, smothered by the tree's
sad and soothe-searching-for-the-child, the worry.

Me, Nucleus, sleep, sees the toddler naked,
with the strange-knowing how acute the riot,
when she slithers out the lapsed door, uncaged,
disturbs into a blunder, out her cot,
watches wise and wounded, enjoys to bury.

Me, Nucleus, sleep, sees the skate-boarder
swish-swash the hazard tarmac street,
taunt odd behaviour at cars that lord-it-over,
dribbling disdain in skid-marks, keen to keep
her glory constant in this scene, above this traffic flurry.

Me, Nucleus, sleep, see the hobby-bobby's
knocked-off hat, some skirmish
where some cruel kids' gormless gang robbed me,
and some rich polite youth, cool and churlish
re-claimed his football, caked in slurry.

Me, Nucleus, sleep, bright-yellow-blindingly and proud,
buzz silently like the sun, roars hope-hidden Leo,
not so eternal as not-one-day-to-burn-away the crowd
that echoes round a body bound to serve its Trio-
kin: see body, soul and spirit sticking close like this, makes
merry.

Me, Nucleus, Sleep.

In Our Prisons

Unknowing, yet thinking that I know,
fat rucksack packed
with rules and tricks and myths,
with tent and pegs and pots,
I stumbled near

got hooked.   Got laid.

Got trapped.

The books I read did not prepare for this.
The crucifix that follows from the kiss.

I think now of those in torment locked,
confined by splints to curb soul's split.

See aborted sages abandoned like a stone.

Or holy gourds, whose hollowness
replete instead
with serpent spin —

too vulnerable to separate within.
Too dislocate no sutra to make kin.

And so...

Seduced and sick — yet thinking that they know

— oh yes —
like most of us,

the 'other' has simply failed to grow.

We Don't Know Why

She's bpd, she splits, she kicks,
so don't get close in case she fits
don't touch, don't talk, keep well away
or sparks will fly to great affray.

She's bpd, her moods swing wide
but never fear she'll suicide
for Bpd's just want attention
and never have a real intention.

She's bpd, abused from birth
her personality was hurt
so now we bash her into shape
to show she's 'wrong' we show her hate.

She's bpd, I'll tell you plain
don't be too kind or be too lame
ensure your boundaries are firm
control her moves at every turn.

She's bpd, a waste of space
they do not have a human trace
they use our resources till dry
and don't improve; we don't know why.

Strange Meeting

Saint Mark sprang like a greyhound, a flash
from some mind-blown trap. Fire tumbled; whirled
within worlds in a frolic upturned as a gentle lash
of love, long longed-for.

Stark words burned the brain, lightning new-born,
clutter cleared like an iron's hot strike; ancient
black-on-white hieroglyphs, sheets uncrumpled at dawn,
and a priest purifies the putrid air.

Bright baptism rivers through the teenage dynamo,
startled and fused, as Catherine wheels sparkle; eyes
stare at you, seeing Jesus' heart and body's blood flow,
making snow-white their heir.

Sixteen years too young to marry pain with such peace,
the truth of universes infinitely far and deep; guilt-time
done, and God-doings clocked Eternity for me, at least,
and the rest was, is, history...

Fair Game

So, if I die: the death of this,
dive down the wormhole,
the idea is-----
to be born again.... What if, instead,
I lose my soul?   What if this mess
you blame of my own making, merely
releases you of taking
care, of being sensitively there?
And all this just and righteous hate,
this muddled stench from cruel and cank'rous
stake, struck through my heart----
(creates such putrid farts),
that remonstrates robots till they crack
and break,
what then? As you ignore,
without you to attack with fiery filial love,
to move and seek to prove unkind intent
was ever meant
way back... You, dumb.   You screw me up.
I suck my thumb. I rock my cot.
And I bemoan this dreadful luck---
whereby my death marries my mum's,

no matter any patient's pain---
Least mine.
And your bereavement leaves no stain.
For a psychoanalyst, you are,
and I'm fair game.

Pilgrim: Scenes & Unseens

(after T.S.Eliot)

I don't, but the soul knows
why the cars' hum back-drop, 3D African Violet,
layers to the wolf's howl
which circles, and the drum, drumming afar
time-out the doomed sage.

I don't, but the soul knows.
Why askew-view, her shoulders shrugged, limbs crucifixed,
legs buckled, sits, sunk in red, hard earth. Glows,
the prowler, eyes transfixed.

I don't, but the soul knows,
why we see my care plan stop,
and you say see, will be okay: keep close,
and leave the clues to me.

I don't, but the soul knows
sequelae's unravel: flash, dive, spin,
the tense drag of calendar, clock, rows
on rows of upturned bulbs defying Spring.

I don't, but the soul knows
why, still outside the city wall, she bleats
witless; but then, endlessly at odds, the dogs' growl
from their stadium traps, tic-leap for freedom's facade.

I don't, but the soul knows
why the still dance matters; the burn back
to the noble path; how then, the wise yield to fate, flows
through summer's portal, this heaven's glory,

only to crescendo
in the rumble of wings.

Masters Of The Universe

They talk about 'opportunity'
whilst I think about
the excitement of existence.
And really, I just want 'to be'.
They want me to have a goal, an ambition
— so I enrol —
for lesson after lesson
To shore myself up against dissolution,
and shame,
and inferiority.

But the syllabus is nonsense.

Then they point, prise or purchase,
push to make me
jump when they say jump,
— But I stumble or teeter my responses,
or mumble my answers
half-heartedly,
with indecisive commitments to the journey:
green then red, then red, then green
And back again....

So,
I became no professor,
No CEO or famous celebrity.
No pompous politician,
anal-retentive
to pursue the most potent 'memes'
whilst undercover the squeeze
pours putrid from the cracks...

Instead, I just spoke my mind,
remained on welfare, playing blind.

And with my magic white stick,
got kicked about quite a lot.

— But played tag endlessly.
water-ski-id with the Canada geese.
Danced with the mad March hares, free
in the full moon,
joked with the lunatics,
— or ecstatic sometimes,
stayed in bed.

Lucky me.

Secrets That Therapists & Their Security Guards Don't Know

I am not a 'thing' outside your 'clan',
to trifle with or rifle gems you can;
I am a personhood, — no, — more than that,
I am. I am. I am. I am. I am....

I am no less because I'm one of 'them',
I'm not an object to push and poke and cram,
I am a wondrous being, not therapist's stat,
I am. I am. I am. I am. I am....

I'm not some trophy to fulfil your plan,
I'm not some underling who 'also ran',
I am a child of God, — not changeling brat,
I am. I am. I am. I am. I am.

I'm not here just to cathect a better scam,
or fit more neatly between better lines that scan
I haven't come to be a more compliant lamb,
— I'm here because I am. I am. I am.

I wasn't born to sit down whilst you stand,
I wasn't meant to worship all that's bland,
this miracle, this brilliant holograph you'd ban
Is truly what I am,
I am. I AM.

Casting

Mark 4:41: 'Who is this? Even the wind and the waves
obey Him!'

Outrageously,

my Consultant Psychotherapist is insisting on purdah
whilst we both muck-in to mutate
my gangrenous psyche. She claims, further-
more, for any improvement to my fate,
my e-mailing must cease,

and to circumscribe this 'splitting', every 'association'
must confluently present, be weighed and processed,
be available for the gift of her 'interpretation';
and so, I understand, to modify my many frets,
and deal creatively with my 'phantasies',

extraordinarily,

my Consultant psychotherapist is insisting on purdah:
that I renounce these projections' boo-hiss politics;
and to 'introject' her psychic 'object', without soft-sawder,
accept the parameters of Klein's analytics.

And so we can search undistractedly 'The Child's' anxieties,
I must, she says, relinquish 'acting out', turn from 'defence',
confront all fears I would avoid, so come back 'Home',
resolve those conflicts through this kindly 'transference'.
'Let's lift this fallen angel to Heaven's carillon',
she coaxes, clanging the archetypal keys.

Dazzlingly,

my Consultant Psychotherapist is insisting on purdah.

Omkar

Poem for a Psychotherapist

Do you see me?
Not fully, for your retribution shows,
your embrace, conditional, indulgent.
The 'insight' you speak of
soiled by ambition.

Do you see me?
Imagined, not complete, you choose
the fractal, one tier, brute solvent
to force these bits to stick.
Too rough —
you do not listen,
enough.

Do you see me?
No more than some other's muse,
the mirror reflected, burning in the heart,
like being in first, second, third, love.

Illusory, the psyche assumes,
hopes, desires, the prizes then won,
when truly, there is only the One

true harmony, — the rest are merely tunes.

'Our Father'

Or 'Business As Usual'.

Pulpit-powered, the politicians,
like magicians,
inveigle and scan
psyches across the land.

Hungry and haunted,
ancient veils
secrete vaults
— as the made-up Masters
make out
and make off.

The Glee That Letter Bore

At first your name had the kick of a rejection slip
dampening my dreams in an aftershock,
a tsunami frightening the horses, the clip clop
echo retreating as the waters rise, a fatal blip

causing the universe to shudder.

The next occasion I saw your name in print,
the missive laboured its harsh intent,
argued more cogently the reasons sent
before, plus more, your name in dark blue ink

decidedly uneasy with this rudder.

Then further as I plunged to taunt the tide
of world gone wild and child awakening in grief,
time came again when the rut of every reef
I grappled, as oil slicks, shunned me. Denied

a life, my vision sunk in hell.

Again, I asked at midnight for my bread,

and weeks and months, eclipses came and went,
and still the raven stalled. Then almost spent,
word returned, and augured I'd be fed.
I fantasized 'He means me well'.

So fortune just beyond my grasp, we met,
the four-stroke splutter lending doubt,
and my troubled challenges invoked your clout,
your letters bled with threats, put me in debt,

banished once more.

Then, next, past crowded number three,
those months that dragged with penal kick,
another letter, which number this, the click
of these keys can't know now, except they know the glee

that letter bore.

Liberation Psychology

Or

Being Cross

I killed my Father

— the blood is on my hands.

Look! See!

I did it

and

it had to be.

I killed my father

— you see what I have done?

        Oh! But how I cried

        when my father died

— for so did I, his son.

I killed my father

— and wished I hadn't done it.

And yet,
my Father said:

'It will be better
now he's dead,

you must do it more often.'

'STaR' Service

The council support worker
visited us today. I am not sure
even now why. I put to her
that all the recent propaganda

to 'modernise' day services
does not fool us, idiots though officers
who devise these schemes, must dismiss
us as; and like the Chinese pandas

given bones to gnaw, now bamboo's
been burnt and bashed, Won't Do.
I spoke loud, angry, aware of glue-
ears screeching for want of mere bland

clients, patients who'll swallow
every trick strikes a cracked hollow,
the waters seep and pour, like snow
exposed by hellfire. Here I stand

it seems the only one. Where stowed
are they who signed to care for those

who cannot care for selves so well, who chose
these roles yet now along with many hand
us o'er to wolves who feign their plans
are prized? Parrots repeat such terms to fans
and foes alike: repeat, repeat; brainwash rams
through paper print, TV, high places, low, band-

stand projections — as Hitler targeted the sick,
the poor and then the Jews. 'Personalise', fit
to each and every one they shout. From where I sit
the Yellow Star more like, more close to plan.

And 'resource allocate'? 'fairness'? These phrases
sound so bright, sincere, so right, but raises
in my mind fears hard to define, except see stages
directing Westward: sinking, sinking, sinking sands.

Remembering

The trees tremble at the woodcutter's coming,
at the kill of the deer, the grass quivers,
the ants panic, and the fishes fly from rivers.
Only the humans remain unaware. Thumbing

tomes, the professors, eloquent, choke their souls,
addressing sleepy students who doodle, abstractedly,
penned-in by formica'd desks, co-dependent roles,
well-rehearsed down decades, proud intellect's calamity.

A tragedy now reaped in eco-spoil, raped Eden,
as Mind, unchallenged, worth-less than dung of cows,
the farmer, child, painter, or he who tends his garden
more likely touches truth, and indubitably knows

more than Nietzsche's baying and gainsaying, -plumbing
the depths of the deluded Christian silly slaves-
and B. F. Skinner too.   In truth, the 'Lordship' each one
craves.
And Forgets: the trees tremble at the woodcutter's coming.

Chomsky Calling

The blinders drunk-us-in dark cellars
where you find us dull and dreamy stuck
banished from soporific selfish odours
in a culture born from seize the buck

she gouged the guts from hearts and homes
and split our psyches oozing spite
she starved the swathes of soul and soup
till bruised and bound they lost their fight

and still her ruthless machiavel' princes, queens
pursue their dumb-vicious self-same crimes
dismiss, distress and carnage lives
as hyenas pounce on deaf and blind.

Capped

'Ladybird, Ladybird fly away home......'

I see the two-punctata ladybird is in decline,

that though habitat is variable, she seeks shelter from cold and wet

into urban, luke-warm builds,

overwinters in crevices, the odd hinge, the underside of hedges.

The harlequins, I hear, gorge

on them though with distaste it seems. So die, the two-spot will, in time. They say

the Asian breed is eccentric, flamboyant, ruthless, brusque,

mimes manners but in fact, sweeps, strikes and strips

a cold contract kill, like locusts show no mercy.

The children have been asked to muster mobiles (those

that have them), and photo-shoot for fun, these specimens,

sign up to nationwide surveys.

The government botanists

are troubled by this malaise, this threat

to our country's biodiversity, ecology. They say

the money-trees' antlers, bugged and rotten, are being

diminished, stagnating growth harbouring shells

of their former selves.

Leaf-litter jesters before a full moon: dry carcass,

the pity of Guy Fawkes fucked up,
and Armageddon cackles.

I see the two-spot ladybird with swingeing burns
doth clock her wings to a former hour
as she spins with the wind.

Dependency Culture

The Big Six Energy Companies
are now charging excessively
for fear,
for anger,
for jealousy
and for hate.

People are complaining of leaks
untended —

of wastage
and of dangers.

The Government, however,
refuses to put a cap on any of it
because, they say,
this would destroy the benefits
of competition.

Blessing The Mess

Now there is no God
and the sun is old
and soon to die
what will you call gold?

Now there is no God
and no telescopic view
to praise or censure you
what will you do?

Now there is no God
to guide or shield
the child who's cold
can you now be bold?

Now there is no God
and the world is wild
and the hell-bent fires
merely solar flares

throwing fits on our faces
like a witch's wand —
Now there is no God
will you correspond..... ?

Now there is no God?

For Richer, For Poorer

The city pips and clangs
big-bellied and busy
like ship's prow
ploughing and planting. Cool
kids, cute and coxy (like their elders)
cleverly tackle the latest fads
revelling in sudden changes, as
whole classes computed yesterday
which next fantastic toy's a must
and which boy shall be blessed.

The city,
its work's waste discarded
like forgotten playthings
in hot pursuit of my first million, remains languishing
by drains amongst slums and weeds, where
skirmishes of litter lies, emptied cans, beer bottles,
plastic tubs and tubes,
poor relations of Millennium bugs.

The people, many-nationed, pass by,
the rich, the poor, the in-between,

embattled, bruised till life's obscene, beat blindly
through bureaucracy to lift the scene
the city,
hard and ungiving, releases
babies
into fields to flourish or to fall
into an earth which clings and sometimes crushes
governed by machines which may squeeze the life out of you

The city's
rise, births chaos, the violence
of stars too soon struck, shooting
stars which shatter the golden paths
that Whittington dreamt of, yet,
even he found the ground workable.

Fed Up

We have a hole where our hearts should be,
— If truly empty
this would not be a bad thing,
for out of beginningless time
we were, indeed, born.

But that absence is not of a void
out of which the breath of God inspires
initiation.

That absence is the vacuum that instead invites
the thousand devils
that fight
with the darkness,
manifesting the forms that divide
and rule us.

And can we return
to the timeless time?
To the innocence of the virgin
and the blessed destiny?

Or are we so spoilt
we are unable to embrace
our original face?

And our birth and our death
still haunt us
as silhouettes on the stage?

Bored Games

'Foxes have their holes, the birds, their nests, but the Son of
Man hath nowhere to lay his head' — Jesus Christ.

'A finger pointing to the moon' — Buddha.

Unfold the cardboard
and step into the dual.
Then, the archetypal Prince's finger, points
to the goal,
and the Fall —
the retrogressive dyspepsia,
in the gaseous chariot
To the Death
To the Death
of all.

In denial,
that riddle of 'to zero'
quieted by
The 'maya' ensnarement.

The Machiavellian trap,
of even, and only, a 'few good men'

sandwiched betwixt
the makeshift abode —
of the fox's hole —
of the bird's nest —

this is your 'home',
this is 'you',

blazing in the breeze.

Wake up!

My New Weltanschauung

No one told me it was not God,
but Higgs Boson
who smacked me into this Legoland
where mucky Tories
crap on the peasants
like Orwell's pigs.

No one told me it was not God
but fucking FAR more grim,
— that my toyful shrieks of glee
were simply dippy spin,
my carpet colonies,
lead-soldier-bloodied,
and Eton-cocked.

No one told me it was not God,
but black holes and stuff that floats,
fat fascists that rape and suck
and matters dark,
in fact,
lurk in the park.

No one told me it was not God,
that wolves' gobs cruising primary reds,
were foiled by alternative gears of angels,
by worthy prayers and faeries
— these fended me from kiddy-fears
shadowed under the bed.
that's what they said.

No one told me it was not God,
that the terrain was quite so stark,
so Bosch-racking of my psyche,
a black sun without redemption,
such slime, the Big Cold fish,
sunk deep in its belly-trap
for no purpose
but abuse...
To be spewn into the Black Swan's
Gullet,
then later
as part of the Usual Plot,
sanitised and carved up for the
The Royal Feast...

When I found out
I dumped the lot.

Now, my dementia
is selective,
I have stumped these bastards.

I'm Bliss.
I'm magic.
I'm mindless.

I'm Anti-Matter.

Creative Writing With Paul

We connect
between lapses, the synapses
buzz, zig-zag
in the ether

What's going on?

Hesitant, the laughter,
the permitted play
soothing and smoothing

the restless senses mired
in static.

Thought like things
spring, scatter and block,
sterile or sizzling.

We'd like our brains re-wired,
new hardware maybe?

To interface more comfortably
the Google matrix.

Easter Uprising

In November, as pug-pressed to death's mirror,
the sun strikes back, black dangerous dreams,
I dwell on you, my guru. As you smother screams,
my abandoned soul descends to hell, withered

and slinking into anonymity. In moon-lit caves
I crouch, there to fester, full of dread,
castrated by fate, and to Hades wed
for three callous years. Here, no paves

of gold, wishing well as I journey upward.
Here, no human hand to lift, in Maya blurred
and as an orphan, my primeval wails unheard
and every urge to stand, misunderstood.

My stomach, a pit, pregnant with a stone
yet no surgeon skilled to cut my pain away,
my tears, so deep, so strong, too choked to pray
then, limbs too traumatized to even moan.

Comatosed, unnoticed, unheeding of the sun
which blest my cheeks, the Spring upheld me,
softly, slowly, egged me forward, so gently
I barely saw what Forces moved me on.

The Breaking of Bread

Poem for M.P.

Behold: my core.
Please cherish it.
Don't let the chaff intrude
upon the wheat; let

my memory not be sour,
let me bloom in it.
Do not think me a crude
label, doomed in a dog-race bet.

Let me be precious, human; in your
old age, let me be a bit
of your life's work that lifts your mood,
not a scion that disaffects.

Close the door,
Don't slam it.
Let me feel the finitude
as not quite infinite.

Changeling

I am the animalization of God
I move, I vibrate to tunes
that create; my wounds
show the paths I have trod.

I am the animalization of God
quarks dance as if infants
joining the dots, jubilant
as images magick from Hod.

I am the animalization of God
breathing through dreams
of flesh-husking schemes
strangely sneak into this quod.

I am the animalization of God
in solid 3D, I amaze and I shock
no 'thing' — I verb: I think, I take stock,
and I see where I've trod.

I am the animalization of God
hear, now, feel, see me, and know
that I've come here to grow
to prod you with my oddity.

A Buddhist Poem

N   othingness is the essence of everything

A   nd until you have gathered that,

Y   our flowers are lifeless.

Intention-ing

A Buddha's bound to be a rebel,
a bird bounding on the wing,
a buddha is unbounded —
remains unbound — now, —
that's the thing...

So I'm bound to be a Buddha
for the poem and the song —
and you can have your fat bank balance
for I know I can't go wrong...

And I will dig deep for this treasure
that's as blinding as the sun
and I will honour this connection
through roots and branches
broad and long...

And I want to share this magic
and zap this maya chuddah
to reveal this ever-prodding truth
that everyone's a buddha.

So Heaven shall shower upon me
and the earth ensure I stand
whilst this little buddha body
fleshes blessings on your land.

Handy

Horses, like Buddha,
can sleep on their feet.

Their psyches tunnel,
tune in,
multi-toed,
skewer the earth.

Healthing the yin yang
with whispers
tender of ancient unity.

The 'dawn horse'
hoofs now,
big-eyed.

Knows well its measure.

GodSpells

You are so vast
and my hands, so small.
Either the salt fool
dives to taste
the ocean's mystery,
or the mind's belief-cum-doubt
clamours
and reigns,
rooted to harbour's home,
clamped to Canute's
imperialist throne.

Hazards

Was it a mistake?
Not in, not out,
but all this seeing
something
like a haunting
somehow fake
without explanation
maybe never awake
from the dream
without boundaries
yet seemingly moving
through eternity
— a zipped file, with
zero hours,
and a space.

Artless

On that day
there will be no traffic,
but a seer and seen découpage shimmer,
dalliance without veil or screen
streaming High Definition.

Your eyes
will shine
and their secrets sing,

and so will mine.

Immortality

It is so One
and it is so alone,
this home.
Ever and forever
non-dual,
never
any fever,
no fire
of desire
at all.
No thing,
Pristine,
The waves have gone.

Just the solid silence,
gently touching,
cupping
the dance.

Holy Cow Dung

Death, shimmering
endlessly,
eternally,

hope-less
help-less,
dances into me.

The Search For What Is Missing

A Letter

The reason we are not happy and always searching for the magic something, is because we are unwilling to embrace the reality of what we really are.

We look outside ourselves for completion – we look for a person, we look for something to believe in, we look for something to attach to, we look to keeping busy. ANYTHING in fact that will enable us to shield ourselves from the Truth.

Yet the Truth is what actually liberates. The Truth is what the Buddhists call 'Enlightenment'. The Truth is the most powerful and wonderful knowing a human being can ever have flow through them.

Yet society, civilisation appears to need lies. It needs structure that we peep through so that for the most part we are protected from the reality of existence.

It is rather like the 'Don't mention the war' joke, but it is the prohibition of 'Don't mention or come into contact with the Truth.'

Yet this is not some 'thing' that is static but it is the background to the 'ever-changing-ness' of our lives. It is like the sky behind the clouds, in which the clouds abide. It is That which embraces all that exists.

And that reality is also the reality of Consciousness. It is the reality of what you really are. Infinite, Unconditional, all-encompassing and ...Eternal.

It is Truth and it is also Love.

Be that.

Be liberated.

Dianne Aslett, July 2016

Acknowledgments

Thank you to Matt Nunn for his wise advice and guidance, and for providing the liberation, even creatively 'chaotic' environment in which many of these poems have been written, and for helping in their selection for publication. Thanks too, to David Hart, Julie Boden and Judith Tweddle for their skilful tutelage at different points over the past 15 years, based at as many venues!

I would also like to extend my thanks to Mary Haynes, my English teacher, for introducing me to the wonderful medium of poetry, when I was a school girl, which has proved a life-time's passion.

Thanks to Kathryn Azarpay, my publisher, for her inspiring encouragement and enthusiasm, and for all her hard work in materialising this anthology, not least the final sifting through and decision-making regarding the poems published here.

The largest task of this enterprise, has been the hunting and capture of dispersed poetry: archived under beds, soggied in bathrooms, smuggled behind books, dog-eared in pockets, twisted up drainpipes.

So, thanks too, to Stephen, for all his patient assistance in helping me to compile my poems in one place, on computer and memory stick, now at last, home and dry in this publication.

About the Poet

Dianne was raised and educated in Surrey before moving to the Midlands where she has spent most part of her adult life. She is a graduate of the University of Southampton, and former teacher of English and drama in North Warwickshire and Cambridgeshire. In this, her first collection, Dianne's interest in the political world, her passion for psychology, philosophy, spirituality and compassion in mental health is self-evident.